CRACKING THE CODE

TO ANSWERED

PRAYERS

14 Proven Steps to See Results in your Prayer Life

Michael Taylor

All scripture references in this text are quoted from the King James Version (KJV) of the Bible, unless otherwise specified.

Cover design and images: Geek Resource Centre, Daniel's Complex, 18 Sydenham Commercial Complex, Saint Catherine, Jamaica

Printed in Jamaica, W.I.
Published by AV Media
Kingston, Jamaica.
www.avmediamanagement.com

For copies of this book and speaking engagements, contact the author:
moreofgodministries@gmail.com or mykalmalachi@gmail.com

Acknowledgements

It is with great privilege that I take this opportunity to thank my Lord and Saviour Jesus Christ for calling me into purpose. I thank God for Bishop Courtney McLean and First Lady Nadine Mclean for their commitment to coach and train me in the way I am to be. I thank the Ministers of Worship and Faith International Fellowship (WAFIF) who are great guardians of my spiritual development.

Thank you, to the love of my life Alicia Taylor, who has been my support and strength. Thank you, my love, for seeing beyond and before what God had placed in me. I honour my parents for their labour and continuous support towards fuelling my growth into being a nation-changer. Special thanks to my Publisher Angelique Virtue for her passion towards building God's kingdom. To all partners, well-wishers and friends, I do not have enough words to say how much I thank you for believing in me.

Introduction

I have visited many churches and have discovered, that many Christians are praying but are not getting results. Many people are praying but are not hearing from God. Therefore, it has been laid on my heart to help people to get the results that I get when I pray. When I pray the sick is healed, and when I pray money shows up in numerous ways. When I pray I hear from God.

It was in 1998 that I began my Christian journey at a small church called Heritage Independent Baptist Church on Old Harbour Road, Spanish Town, St. Catherine. I was only a teenager when I got saved but I had a real love for God and the things of God. Along this journey I prayed almost every day, but it wasn't until I discovered certain principles that I began to get serious results. In this book, I have outlined some key principles, based in biblical teaching, explaining how to get answered prayers. I learnt these key principles from my own personal walk with God and from listening to sermons at my home church, Worship and Faith International Fellowship.

I believe that when you read this book and apply the principles outlined therein to your life, you will get serious results. I declare that your understanding will open up and your prayer life will excel to new levels in God. I declare that as you read this book and apply these principles you will become a prayer warrior for the kingdom of God. I declare that your prayer life will cause your destiny to become your reality in due season and that its impact will cause the kingdom of heaven to be advanced to its optimum in the earth, in Jesus Name.

Table of Contents

Code #1 – **Use the Template**

PRAY THE LORD'S PRAYER

Jesus gave the template of how to get answered prayers in Matthew Chapter 6.

Matthew 6:9-16 *"After this manner therefore pray ye: Our Father which art in heaven, Hallowed be thy name. Thy kingdom come, Thy will be done in earth, as it is in heaven. Give us this day our daily bread. And forgive us our debts, as we forgive our debtors. And lead us not into temptation, but deliver us from evil: For thine is the kingdom, and the power, and the glory, for ever. Amen."*

ACKNOWLEDGEMENT (Our Father which art in heaven, Hallowed be thy name)

If you are delivering a package, it is important to put the address on it. If there is no address, anyone can open it when it is being delivered. If you are sending a message to God, it is important to address your message to God correctly in order for your message to reach the throne room. I believe this was what Jesus was teaching us when He taught us to pray by saying *"Our father who art in heaven hallowed be thy name."* He was teaching us how to get the Father's attention.

The Greek word for hallowed is *hagiazō* which means to acknowledge. How can you ask anything from God without first acknowledging him? How would you feel if you were a king and someone entered into your throne room without first acknowledging you? How you acknowledge your God will determine if you get his attention.

No king will give you a listening ear until you acknowledge his presence, until you recognize his superiority. Think about making a telephone call without dialling the number. It would be impossible for you to do. In the same way, we have to learn how to dial into heaven and when we are sure that a connection is made, then we make our requests.

HIS KINGDOM AND HIS WILL (Thy kingdom come, Thy will be done in earth, as it is in heaven.)

Whenever we get God's attention he teaches us to place his kingdom first. In other words, how can the kingdom be built through you? If God should bless you will you remember his kingdom? We should pray that his kingdom should be established through us in every way possible and that his will be done. This means that what we ask should exalt and promote the agenda of God. Whatever we ask should be representative of God's personality and demonstrative of his power.

PROVISION (Give us this day our daily bread.)

We should not be afraid to ask for provision. In fact, the very air we breathe is supplied by God. Since He is the source of everything, we must recognize our dependency on Him. One of the benefits of a good father is that he is a provider. Our heavenly father does this very well, in fact better than any earthly father! God wants to provide for us, so spend time asking.

FORGIVENESS (And forgive us our debts, as we forgive our debtors.)

We all will have sins to be forgiven. How can we expect to be forgiven if we have not forgiven. As we forgive others our Father forgives us. Asking for forgiveness and committing to forgive others demonstrates our humility and our acknowledgement of our flaws. It reminds us that God is the righteous judge and establishes his ultimate, divine, pardoning power.

PROTECTION AND PREVENTION (And lead us not into temptation, but deliver us from evil:)

Who can protect us like God? Who indeed can deliver us from evil? Only God! Especially since the devil is seeking whom he may devour (1 Peter 5:8) we should never leave out asking for God protection. Others may seek other means, and believe that they are guarded against evil. But only the coverage of God is true. As we pray, we acknowledge the ultimate power of God and reject the quasi power of other forces. In Job 2:2 we see where Satan confessed walking to and forth in the earth. He is seeking to cause you and I to falter but the prayers of the saint can counter-attack every planned evil attack. Therefore it is important to pray for avoidance of temptations.

THANKSGIVING AND REVERENCE (For thine is the kingdom, and the power, and the glory, for ever. Amen.)

At the end of each prayer we must express reverence and thankfulness to our Lord for the power He possesses to answer our prayers and His willingness to hear our prayers. For this cause we bless and adore Him. End your prayers with worship and thanksgiving knowing that the Lord has heard your requests.

The Dakes Annotated Reference Bible gives 23 elements to the Lord's Prayer. The first three petitions make seven points concerning God and the last four petitions make 16 points concerning man. This is to heighten your understanding of how to steer your prayers towards effectiveness.

Relationship: Our Father
Recognition: which art in heaven
Adoration: Hallowed be thy name
Anticipation: Thy kingdom come
Consecration: Thy will be done
University: in earth
Conformity: as it is in heaven
Supplication: Give us
Definiteness: this day
Necessity: our daily bread
Penitence: And forgive us
Obligation: our debts
Forgiveness: as we forgive
Love and mercy: our debtors
Guidance: And lead us
Protection: not into temptation
Salvation: but deliver us
Righteousness: from evil
Faith: For thine is the kingdom
Humility: and the power
Reverence: and the glory
Timelessness: for ever
Affirmation: Amen

Code #2 – **Repent**

PRAY THE SINNERS PRAYER

Are you a child of God? If you are not a son, or a daughter, how can you say *"Our Father"*? Jesus designed the Lord's Prayer for His children. It is His children that are entitled to His benefits and if you are a child of God, whatever you desire, within the will of God, belongs to you. But if you have not yet repented, you have been blocked from the benefits of God by sin.

John 9:31 *"Now we know that God heareth not sinners: but if any man be a worshipper of God, and doeth his will, him he heareth."*

This is not to condemn you but it is to give you the opportunity to reap the rewards of God. Below I have outlined the sinners' prayer. Repeat it with a sincere heart and you will be saved. Thereafter find a Bible believing church that helps you grow in the faith. Thereafter, your life will never be the same.

Romans 10:9 *"That if thou shalt confess with thy mouth the Lord Jesus, and shalt believe in thine heart that God hath raised him from the dead, thou shalt be saved."*

Salvation Prayer
"Lord Jesus I am a sinner, forgive me of my sins and come into my heart. Save me, deliver me, set me free from this day forward, in Jesus name, Amen.

Code #3 – **His Will, not yours**

PRAY GOD'S WILL

Matthew 6:10 *"Thy kingdom come, Thy will be done in earth, as it is in heaven."*

Notice the order of the prayer that Jesus prayed. He prayed the fathers will to come before praying for provision or anything else. Train your mind to always remember that it is God's will that you are here to fulfill. The Bible says *"For whom he did foreknow, he also did predestinate to be conformed to the image of his Son, that he might be the firstborn among many brethren."* (Romans 8:29).

Allow your fleshly desires to die and give way to the Holy Spirit to control your life. You are not a goat but a sheep and God designed you to be a follower of Him. Nothing will be truly successful and lasting in your life until you follow the Father's will. Know your God-given purpose. That is where success lies.

I am able to write this book, only because I am fulfilling His will. All I had planned to do in life was to sit around a computer and do programming or graphics. But that was not His will. It was when I began to pray His will that God shifted my life into what I am today. Never allow the world to define you. Allow what God says about you to take full effect and be your foundation definition.

Don't be ashamed to be detailed to God. For example, if you are married, or seeking to be married, pray God's will as it relates to who to marry and about your marriage, and it will help you to say married. Yes, you will have challenges, but when you remember that God said that this is the one, you will not easily jump out of the marriage.

Pray God's will as it relates to your next business investment or job opportunity. Pray God's will as it relates to which church to attend, which school or degree programme to enrol into. Diligently do this, for when God's will prevails, success will be easy and peace of mind will come. Never allow your emotions to take the place of the Holy Spirit in determining how to live out the Christian journey.

Code #4 – **You, Yourself and God**

PRAY IN SECRET

Matthew 6:6 *"But thou, when thou prayest, enter into thy closet, and when thou hast shut thy door, pray to thy Father which is in secret; and thy Father which seeth in secret shall reward thee openly."*

Your secret place blocks out distractions and helps you to focus on God. Nothing is wrong with praying in church or with groups or even with friends. But it is your private time with God that will reveal the secret things of God. No matter how much you pray with others, ensure that you spend a part of your day praying alone to God.

Your alone time will blow your enemy's mind when they see how much you shine through tests and trials. It is the covenant commission of every Christian to have secret time with God. It is your secret time that will bring your greatest reward. This is an area in which believers are often attacked. Often, our earthly duties are the tools used to interfere with the spiritual mandate of intimacy with God through personal prayer.

We must guard against this trend, since, it is your secret time with God that ensures excellence in your earthly pursuits. Your secret time will help you to unlock strategies of how to manage your family, resolve issues on the job, how to minister to people, how to live this life. Don't let a day pass without spending your alone time with God praying and reading His Word. It will change your life.

Code #5 – **Respect Due**

HONOUR GOD

1 Chronicles 4:9-10 NLT *"There was a man named Jabez who was more honorable than any of his brothers. His mother named him Jabez because his birth had been so painful. He was the one who prayed to the God of Israel, "Oh, that you would bless me and expand my territory! Please be with me in all that I do, and keep me from all trouble and pain!" And God granted him his request."*

Jabez was more honourable than all his brothers which means that there was something that Jabez was doing that his other brothers were not doing. I am pretty sure that just like every other man on this earth, Jabez's brothers had prayer requests too. So why is it that God answered Jabez's requests? I submit to you that because Jabez was more honourable than all his brothers, God honoured him above his same brothers.

The Bible teaches us, *"for them that honour me I will honour, and they that despise me shall be lightly esteemed."* (1 Samuel 2:30b). Your honour level determines your prosperity level. If you want God to honour you, you will have to learn to honour him. If you want God to answer your prayers you will have to learn to answer His requests.

Just like money is a currency here on earth used for the exchange of goods and services. Honour is a currency that operates out of heaven. If you honour God and the things of God, then God is moved and persuaded to honour you.

9

God's requests are often difficult and challenging in the human eye. However, the rewards of honouring God's requests are priceless.

The Bible says, *"Honour the Lord with thy substance, and with the firstfruits of all thine increase: So shall thy barns be filled with plenty, and thy presses shall burst out with new wine."* (Proverbs 3:9-10)

I remember giving God my first, even when I was in debt up to my neck. After releasing, I have seen God's uncommon blessings and favour bestowed upon my life. How often is it that someone walks up to you and says, the Lord says I should give you money towards your housing and every month they actually come and give that money? How often is it that someone comes up to you and says the Lord says I should give you a car? How often is it that you are in need of furniture and someone comes and says I am going to give you some furniture? How often is it that someone pays for your car insurance without you even asking? How often is it that someone just buys you gas without even asking? How often is it that when you go into the supermarket someone pays for your groceries? Do your bills get paid supernaturally? When you get your bills have you ever seen 'paid' on the receipt? All these and more are ways in which my God has honoured me because I have honoured him.

Wow! I can't explain how much I love serving Jesus! When you honour God, He is compelled to honour you! I believe there are some unexpected miracles waiting to be released in your life if you learn to honour God. Do you believe you are giving God your best? Examine yourself and ask yourself, "Am I really honouring God?" This is a question we must constantly ask ourselves. We must thrive to ensure that the spirit of religiosity doesn't take us captive, where we become merely church-goers with no relationship with God. We must ensure that the things of this world and our loved ones do not take the place of God

Code #6 – **Let it Go!**

FORGIVE AND FORGIVE QUICKLY

Matthew 6:14-15 *"For if ye forgive men their trespasses, your heavenly Father will also forgive you: But if ye forgive not men their trespasses, neither will your Father forgive your trespasses."*

If you don't delete junk from your phone, after a while it will cease to function. Too many people carry unforgiveness, and this blocks what God wants to release in their lives. The law of receiving is giving. If you give forgiveness you will receive forgiveness. Not letting go of an individual is not causing them harm, instead it causes you harm. Your heart is a place where God lives but he cannot thrive where there is unforgiveness.

A man came to me once, saying the Lord had sent him to me for a word concerning some money a man had owed him for years. The man was in tears heartbroken after what he had been through trying to get back his money from this man for years. Immediately the Lord spoke to me and said tell him to forgive the man and let it go. When I told the man what the Lord said, he was distraught! He thought I was going to command angels to arrest his debtor and command his funds to be returned. But his answer to his prayer was simply letting his debtor go. Forgiveness was the key to unlock the money he was waiting to be returned to him and I guarantee you that if he had let it go, God would show up with double of what he was looking for. As the Bible says, forgive quickly (Col 3:13 MSG). Situations are bound to arise that challenge our command to forgive, but if you learn to let go quickly, you will never be separated from your Father and His benefits.

If you really find it hard to forgive, spend some time praying for that individual. Pray that they would find salvation and hurt no one else. Pray, asking God for grace to let it go. I guarantee you that if you sincerely pray, God will help you to let it go.

Code #7 – **Don't Stop!**

PRAY FERVENTLY

James 5:16-17 *"Confess your faults one to another, and pray one for another, that ye may be healed. The effectual fervent prayer of a righteous man availeth much. Elias was a man subject to like passions as we are, and he prayed earnestly that it might not rain: and it rained not on the earth by the space of three years and six months."*

The definition for the word fervent is actually *energeō* which means to be operative, be at work, put forth power. If you want serious results, you must apply energy to your prayers. It is not that God is deaf. It is the fact that the answers to your prayers are being contended for. Some prayers need intensity. It is like a woman giving birth, you have to wrestle until there is a release. I believe that it was something akin to this that happened to Jesus as he prayed on the mountain before His crucifixion (Luke 22:44). I have always wondered, how is it that he was sweating on a mountain, early in the morning when was so cold? It was the intensity of His prayer that caused him to sweat the way he did!

If Christ can be fervent, so can you! How desperate are you to receive what you are believing God for? If you are desperate enough, I challenge you to position yourself like Elijah when he heard the sound of abundance of rain, and begin to pray until there is a release (1Kings 18:41-45).

I remember when my life was in 'pause'. Nothing was happening. I knew I was talented and smart, but a Spirit was suppressing me. I remember going to a fasting service and crying out to God. Some persons must have thought that I was crazy, but I didn't care. Even after church I still felt an urgency to pray. I remember leaving church and returning in the night to pray again. This time it was louder and more intense. It was necessary at the time to defeat the devils plaguing my life. I wanted to go forward in life but nothing was moving. I wanted a job, I wanted to enter into a purposed life, but nothing was moving. I recognized the true meaning of fervent praying after that day because immediately after that things began to turn in my life.

Some prayers require this kind of approach. Fervency stretches our faith and gets heaven's response. This faith compels and strengthens you to pray until something happens. Take a look at Luke Chapter 18 and you will find the widow and the unjust judge. However, it is verse 7 and 8 that stands out to me. *"And shall not God avenge his own elect, which cry day and night unto him, though he bear long with them? I tell you that he will avenge them speedily. Nevertheless when the Son of man cometh, shall he find faith on the earth?"*

Shall not God avenge you? Notice the key word "cry". These are not average prayers! The Greek translation for cry is *boao* which means to 'hallo or shout for help in tumultuous way'. Do you really want help? Begin to shout for help assiduously. Passivity won't work here. This requires a true utterance for the relief of pain. This requires brokenness. This asks us to get to that place where you recognize that only God can resolve the matter at hand. If there are other options in your head you have not reached desperation yet! If you are too tired or cannot find the time, you are not needy enough! There must be an urgency, an expressed and demonstrated hunger for an encounter, a desperation for a manifestation - then there will be a release.

Code #8 – **Speak His Language**

PRAY IN THE SPIRIT

1 Corinthians 14:2 *"For he that speaketh in an unknown tongue speaketh not unto men, but unto God: for no man understandeth him; howbeit in the spirit he speaketh mysteries."*

The gift of tongues has been given to help us to communicate with heaven. Notice the Bible says that when we speak in tongues we speak to God and not to man because no man can fathom God. We don't have enough words in our vocabulary to say things that we need to say to God. Therefore in order to help with our imperfections, God gives us heavenly languages and the Holy Spirit speaks on our behalf.

I was limited in my communication to God until I began to speak in other tongues. It is the most critical ingredient to make your prayer life soar. Paul says in Corinthians 2, *"For what man knoweth the things of a man, save the spirit of man which is in him? Even so the things of God knoweth no man, but the Spirit of God* (v11).

Therefore, when we speak in tongues, we are allowing the spirit of God in us to communicate the things that we are incapable of saying to God. God knows our future and he knows what he wants to do on earth and no one can read God's mind but the Spirit of God who knows God's mind. Therefore, don't be fooled by some theologians that tell you that you shouldn't use your heavenly gift. If God didn't want us to use the gift, then why did he give it to us? Your gift is to edify you, making you a better prayer warrior, one who gets serious results.

As for me, I believe my strongest spiritual gift is prayer, and my second strongest is the gift of 'word of knowledge'. The question to ask however, is how do I get to the place where, when I show up I am accurate in word of knowledge? How do I prophecy accurately? How do I get these manifestations when I minister? I fast and pray indeed, but it is not all the time that I fast. My most successful ministry in Word happens after having prayed in tongues for a great while before coming into the service.

Sometimes I turn my car into a prayer machine – tongues, tongues, tongues until I arrive at the place of ministry. It is as if I am downloading a file from heaven for the manifestation ahead. The more I am effective in my concentrated time of praying in tongues, the more confident and accurate I am. If you want to get better results, when you pray, begin to use your heavenly language and you will be shocked by the manifestations.

During my early Christian life, I was taught not to speak in tongues without an interpreter. But as I grew in the faith, I gained more understanding of what Paul was saying. The Corinthian church was using tongues with no words that were communicable to the audience. They were trying to preach in tongues, showing off their language. This indeed makes no sense at all but it doesn't negate the use of tongues in church.

However, in your personal prayer time, use tongues as often as you receive utterance, as, it is in those moments that the Holy Spirit speaks to heaven for you, and petitions for you concerning things even you know not. I implore you to ask God to baptize you with cloven tongues of fire even if you already have the gift. Ask for more and you will be shocked by the results you achieve.

Code #9 – **Where Two or Three**

PRAY WITH A PRAYER PARTNER

Acts 16:25-26 *"And at midnight Paul and Silas prayed, and sang praises unto God: and the prisoners heard them. And suddenly there was a great earthquake, so that the foundations of the prison were shaken: and immediately all the doors were opened, and every one's bands were loosed."*

I don't believe Paul could do it without Silas or Silas without Paul. There is a level you need to climb to and it is aided by praying with someone else. There is a level that you need to unlock but you will need someone to agree with you. No wonder the Bible says, *"Two are better than one; because they have a good reward for their labour. For if they fall, the one will lift up his fellow: but woe to him that is alone when he falleth; for he hath not another to help him up."* (Ecclesiastes 4:9-12). There is a battle to win, there is a devil to be defeated, there is a prison to break out of, but you may not be able to do it without someone else with you.

When you pray with someone else, it gives you energy, especially if the person you are praying with is a better prayer warrior than you. In my early days of prayer it was my weekly visits to fasting services praying with Minister Angela Headly, that helped me to grow in prayer. Every Thursday morning she would pray for one hour and for that hour I would push in prayer as she pushes in prayer.

Glory be to God! This training helped me to become who I am today. You will never become a strong prayer warrior until you push pass a certain level. If the longest you have ever prayed is 15 minutes you will never be able to pray for an hour easily.

I challenge you to find somebody to pray with you that is stronger than you. Your level in prayer will increase. A good ground for this is an all-night prayer meeting and prayer with the congregation and the minister leading. This training ground will push you past a certain limit and once you have gotten to that milestone it will be easier for you to reach it again.

Code #10 – **Over and Over Again!**

PRAY CONSISTENTLY

1 Thessalonians 5:17 *"Pray without ceasing."*

One great man said a little every day, is better than a whole lot someday. It is better to pray at various time intervals throughout the day than to struggle to spend a lot of time all at once. If you allow a dripping pipe to leak on a solid floor, after a while, there will be a huge puddle of water. When you pray with consistency, your prayers are penetrating the walls of the enemy. Daniel prayed three times a day and that's why, when he was thrown in the lion's den, the lions couldn't touch him. Daniel's consistency in prayer caused angels to protect him consistently.

"My God hath sent his angel, and hath shut the lions' mouths, that they have not hurt me: forasmuch as before him innocency was found in me; and also before thee, O king, have I done no hurt." (Daniel 6:22)

I challenge you to resist complacency and push for the greater glory. Paul said, *"I press towards the mark of the higher calling..."* (Phil 3: 14). Pray without ceasing, for your prayers are being recorded (Revelation 5:8) and every prayer you pray, puts your assigned angels to work. The Bible says, *"And he spake a parable unto them to this end, that men ought always to pray, and not to faint;"* (Luke 18:1). When you stop praying you lose faith in receiving what you are believing for. Consistency will always defeat the enemy. Challenge yourself to be consistent by setting alarms and being accountable to others.

Engage others and pray for them while forgetting about your problems. Join the intercessory team if you need a boost or visit the fasting service. It is as simple as this: Plan your life with Jesus in it and that will help you to become consistent. My wife says even in my sleep I am praying. It is because prayer has now become my lifestyle. I pray about anything and everything. May that grace come upon your life, in Jesus' name.

Code #11 — **A Time for Everything**

PRAY AT THE HOUR OF PRAYER

Acts 3:1 *"Now Peter and John went up together into the temple at the hour of prayer, being the ninth hour."*

While God operates out of time man operates in time and there are set times that heaven communicates with earth. God is omnipresent, however God is still the creator of time and he appreciates and honours when you set times to meet with him.

I believe there is a special reason why Peter and John went up to the temple at a certain time. When you take hold of these practices of set times of prayer, as honoured by great men like David and Daniel, you will get serious results. Set dedicated times to pray to God, and honour them. In the book of Psalms the Bible says, *"Evening, and morning, and at noon, will I pray, and cry aloud: and he shall hear my voice."* (Psalms 55:17) David prayed at the hours of prayer and we can attest to the good relationship that David had with God. We know further, that he got serious results from God.

I remember while I was working in the banking sector, I had reminders at the hours of prayer to pray. While I was working at my desk I prayed under my breath in tongues each time I got the reminders. This reminder helped me to connect with God consistently and this strengthened my relationship with God. When I prayed at these times, I felt fire on my hands. God was assuring me of His presence. It helped to keep me charged with God's presence to face life's daily duties. I remember at an hour of prayer I was praying and suddenly I began to hear a conversation in a totally different place. At the end of the work day while I was going home, the Spirit of the Lord lead me to a detour and when I arrived to a specific place, I saw the manifestation of the exact conversation I had heard from my desk!

There is so much to achieve in God if you learn to apply these principles. God was preparing me for the work ahead. While I communicated with God at the hours of prayer, it connected me to God at a deeper, more intimate level. Today, I believe that is why I am able to hear from God so clearly.

I challenge you now, to begin to pray at the hours of prayer and watch what God will do in your life. You will be naturally supernatural when you challenge yourself to pray at these hours.

Code #12 – I Know What I Know

PRAY WITHOUT DOUBTING

Matthew 7:8-9 *For every one that asketh receiveth; and he that seeketh findeth; and to him that knocketh it shall be opened. Ask, and it shall be given you; seek, and ye shall find; knock, and it shall be opened unto you*

Doubt is one of man's biggest problems and when we doubt, we fail to understand the capabilities of the God we serve. The Bible says, *"without faith it is impossible to please God"* (Hebrews 11:6) and depending on your level of faith, it will determine how much God will release in your life. If you are only believing God for a one bedroom he will only give you a one bedroom but if you are believing God for a two story house with a Jacuzzi and a double car port, a pool, a balcony, guest room, dining room, a theatre, a powder room, a tennis court, a games room, a gym; well that will be your portion, and more! Ask and it shall be given to you, make your request and allow God to do the rest.

I remember just before we got married, Alicia - my wife - and I were looking for a house. We began to walk through a community we loved. We didn't have much money to pay rent and we didn't even have furniture. Faith is what we had. I remember us soon finding a house, but it was way past our budget. The following morning I woke up with Genesis chapter 18 in my head and when I read through the chapter the verse that says, *"Is there anything too hard for God?"* (v14) jumped out at me. God was helping us to believe. How ironic is it that, the day after we had literally packed bags and moved by faith, God gave me a dream about his possibilities. This lifted our faith and that very week, someone committed to giving us approximately 20% of the amount we needed every month towards our rent. To God be the Glory! When you pray don't limit God. Don't limit his capabilities. If you have doubts, pray still, and ask God to take away your doubt and increase your faith. By confessing your doubt, God will honour your vulnerability and comfort you by demonstrating his power!

I pray for you that you too will get a dream, a word, a touch or some other sign from heaven that will increase your faith, in Jesus name.

Code #13 – **Double-time!**

PRAY AND FAST

Matthew 17:21 *"Howbeit this kind goeth not out but by prayer and fasting."*

This is where my Christian life changed from ordinary to extra-ordinary. I learnt to fast and pray. It was the help of my spiritual father Bishop Courtney McLean that brought transformation to my life. I was just an average church goer when I met Bishop and I was looking for a job for about two years when he gave me a book on fasting. After reading it, I entered into three days of prayer and fasting that turned my life around for good. I have never regressed since then. My life has kept itself on an endless upward trajectory.

I learnt that prayer and fasting is a Christian's secret weapon and that if you learn to use this weapon well, no trials can take advantage of you. There are certain devils that will not be defeated with prayer only. It is the combination of both prayer and fasting that will cause a greater level of anointing to come upon you and begin to flow through you. If you want to operate *naturally supernatural*, you will have to fast and pray so that the Glory of the Lord will come upon your life.

Just imagine pouring gasoline on an open flame. This is what happens when you fast and pray. The Bible says He makes His ministers *a flaming fire* (Heb 1:7). Just imagine gas being added to a flame you currently carry. The devils you are facing will consider you too hot for them. You will be too hot to be tormented and your level or relationship with God will explode to new dimensions.

I remember fasting and praying for 40 days and everything in my life turned for good. My ministry exploded not because of eloquence in speech but because of the glory and power I carried. This caused me to lose friends because I was operating at a different level and some friends I had didn't want to be friends with me anymore. My marriage was upside down but after this fast, every spell that was cast against my marriage was broken. My finances went to a new place too. In fact, I didn't have a car, and it was right after this fast that someone gave me a car. Blessings multiplied non-stop because of what I released in the spiritual realm when I fasted and prayed.

I wonder what is waiting to be released in your life. I challenge you to make a sacrifice that you have never made before and God will have no choice but to bless you like He has never blessed you before.

Code #14 – **One and Ready, Two and Move!**

PRAY, THEN MOVE BY FAITH

Jesus went up into the mountain to pray, but after praying He came down doing miracles, signs and wonders (Matthew 8:1-3). Many intercessors are unsuccessful because after all their praying they do nothing at all. Your miracle will be activated through your faith actions. What are faith actions? They are actions that you do in faith.

Remember, Alicia and I had no money but we moved by faith after praying towards getting a house. I remember when we needed a car we went to a car sales promotion event and signed up to buy a car. While we were at the event the sales agent asked us which of the cars we were interested in buying. We spoke confidently, selecting the one we wanted as if we had the money to buy it immediately. We even asked for an invoice knowing that we didn't have enough money as yet to buy the car.

While looking at the car, a friend was passing by and saw us and asked which one of the cars we were planning to purchase. We went right ahead and pointed to the one we were planning to purchase, knowing full well that we didn't have enough money to buy the car. The truth is we didn't get to buy that car, but our faith actions led to God's actions concerning us. I believe our faith pleased God and that faith unlocked our blessing. It was only a little while later that someone blessed us with a car. I believe the grace was unlocked to acquire vehicles, and I believe the same and more will be unlocked for you if you believe and act in the name of Jesus.

The system of the world is different from the system of heaven. The world operates by the exchange of money for goods and services. The world operates from what it can touch and see. However, heaven's currency is not money or things. One of heaven's chief currencies is faith. Faith is belief that is proven by actions.

If you truly believe, you would rise up and move toward the thing you asked of God. Your actions must display faith if you plan to receive anything from God. The test of belief is what you do when an impossibility is before you. Do you curse God like the children of Israel trapped between the Red Sea and the Egyptians? Or, do you stretch forth your rod like Moses? I wonder what you have been praying about that God has been waiting to bless you with if you would just move?

YOU NOW HAVE THE CODES!

Prayer is about relationship. When we pray, we speak with our Divine Creator, our God, who desires to know us and to make himself known to us. Prayer is not a transactional arrangement, neither is it a one way stream of requests or of blessings. Prayer draws us close to our good Father and gives us access to a relationship that is hinged on love and is maintained by faith. God is waiting with excitement and a deep longing not to answer you only, but to get to know you and to then demonstrate His love to you as you commune.

God tells us that he will give us the desires of our heart (Psalm 37:4). May you seek God in prayer only as inspired by His own desires placed in your heart. May He answer you in the natural as your relationship grows in the spiritual. So pray, my brothers and sisters, pray always and fervently. Then, after praying, move towards that house that God has already prepared for you. Move towards that business that is waiting on the manager inside of you to arise. After praying, prepare yourself academically to receive that promotion or that job. After praying, go look for properties that have your name on it by faith. Go look for cars that have your name written on the seats, by faith. Expect God to fix that situation that heavily perplexes you. Expect God to heal your diseases. Expect God to show up right now. Expect God to cause something to happen supernaturally.

Pray, believe and move!

www.ingramcontent.com/pod-product-compliance
Lightning Source LLC
Chambersburg PA
CBHW071759020426
42331CB00008B/2321